Journey

Writings by

Dennis M. Stanfield

© 2008 Dennis M. Stanfield

Copyright Page

ISBN: 978-0-615-26495-0

© 2008 Dennis M. Stanfield

Publication Date: 10/2008
Release Date: November 30, 2008

Book Design by Lulu.com and Dennis M. Stanfield

For more information and other books please visit the websites below or email the author directly.

Lulu store front (http://stores.lulu.com/store.php?AcctID=1126042)

http://www.authorsden.com/dennismstanfield

Marc_man_arts@yahoo.com

All rights reserved. None of the content of this publication may be reproduced, resold, redistributed, or transmitted in any form or by any means (electronic, photocopying, recording, or otherwise) with out prior written permission of the author/publisher.

© 2008 Dennis M. Stanfield

Dedication

This book is dedicated to OUR future. Every choice made, effects another person; positive or negative. I pray OUR future is bright.

This book is also dedicated to my grandfather, Tommie Lee Stanfield, Sr.; my great grandfather, William Childress; Mother Gertrude Ribbins; and the rest of my family and close friends. I am still, because all of you are!

I still feel pain when I think of my grandfather and other family I've lost. I know others do as well, so this poem is for me and all of you...

Going Home

Today is a day of sadness, yes
But today is also a day to feel blessed
To feel gracious
Though a part of you may feel spacious
That someone you loved is now painless
Today is a day to rejoice
To lift up your voice
To be proud to be his/her daughter or son
Proud to tell everyone of the good of this person
A person in your life forever or just a moment's time
A person who is about to be in their prime
Because they are walking where there is no time
Where there is no crime
Where the wind blows just to kiss you and the sun always shines
They're in a place you can only imagine
Sad they left you, but what a blessing to have them
Don't be sad, mad or upset when reading/hearing this poem
But be glad, because the one you loved is going home

© 2008 Dennis M. Stanfield

Introduction

Luke 15:13 – And not many days later, the younger son gathered everything together and went on a JOURNEY into a distant country, and there he squandered his estate with loose living. (N.A.S.)

Journey – Any Passage from one stage to another.

I like to write about life. They say life happens in stages, so now I see the connection in calling life a journey. In this book you will read about two journeys that hopefully, you can relate to and enjoy.

One journey is for a young person who can deal in the negatives or positives of life. The person has been dealt a bad hand at this stage in life; but what will be done with it? Put yourself in this position. The "system" is against you, so what can be done with a fixed deck? Will you deal in the negative: Drugs, violence and further desecration of your culture? Or will you deal in the positive: Education, family and the uplifting of your culture? This journey is more personal to me as I move forward to another stage in my life journey.

The second journey is of love. A stage in life everyone goes through and some more than others. Love touches everyone and can be a tough journey all by itself. After making a mistake the journey of love doesn't end between two people; it gains strength. The relationship of love is work and is never promised to be easy. So just look at the positives and see what you can get out of love… ready?

© 2008 Dennis M. Stanfield

Table of Contents

Title Page	1
Copyright Page	2
Dedication	3
Introduction	4
Table of Contents	5
Intro to Dealer	7
Dealer Part I	8
Family	9
Fatherless Father	10
Starts at Home	11
Going Backwards	12
Hardtime, USA	13
Stuck on the Roof	14
Hard	15
Dear America	16
Black Panther	17
Live to Tell	18
Less Than He	19
41	20
In a Flash	21
Gotta Eat	22
Reality	23
She Cries	24
Out	25
Statistic	26
He, She and Them	27
Excuses	28
Justified Anger	29
Surface Dwellers	30
Back My Way	31
Dealer Part II	32
Dealer	33
Poetry Man	34
Brain Storm	35
Complex Thoughts	36
Jesus Is My Man	37
Message in a Bottle	38
My Father's Time	39
Tell 'Em	40
Misunderstood	41
Black Kiss	42
Life Is But a Dream	43
Writing In the Dark	44
Wishing on a Star	45
Past the Stars	46
Scratch	47
M&M	48
Ali	49

© 2008 Dennis M. Stanfield

Table of Contents (Cont.)

Wonder	50
Strings	51
Big Brother	52
The Inspirations of Me	53
All Good Things	54
Intro to Love Story	55
Love Story	56
Roses	57
More Roses	58
Baby	59
What We Had	60
Heartless	61
From a Broken Heart	62
Acquired Taste	63
Rebirth of Love	64
Reminds Me of Her	65
Star	66
Cookie Jar	67
Black Cat	68
Head Lights	69
Redemption Poem	70
Hello, Goodbye	71
Loud Silence	72
Talk To Me	73
Lonely Bed	74
Swallowing Rain	75
Remember Me	76
Kiss Me	77
My Fantasy and I	78
Relax	79
Cool Night	80
Love Air	81
Love Rain	82
In Her Eyes	83
Love Land	84
Sunset	85
Landscape	86
Until (Loving You)	87
Super Friends	88
Thank You's	99

© 2008 Dennis M. Stanfield

Dealer

Everyone wants to be a hustler of sorts. Me, I am a dealer. My culture likes to take negative words and turn them positive; for example, bad meaning good. With that connection I chose Dealer to make positive. Kids look up to the wrong kind of dealer to show them a way out in their bad community. I want them to see a different and more positive way to make it on their own. See the negative others see and see how to change it. I deal in hope and inspiration. I deal in imagination. Books plus your imagination take you to a place of your own making and expand the realms of thought. There is a picture there that you paint in your own mind. The words come to life and become visual. Our kids aren't learning because their minds aren't being flexed. The kids aren't inspired by anything other than the material things. All they need is hope and inspiration. Yes, I'm trying to get you hooked to a product, an idea. Reading is fundamental, don't take it for granted. Follow me...

© 2008 Dennis M. Stanfield

Dealer:

Part I

© 2008 Dennis M. Stanfield

Family

Family is the most important thing
Those people help mold you as a human being
Cousins, uncles, aunts, grandparents tell you right from wrong
When your parents aren't there they keep you strong
I'm blessed to have a strong fam
From the North to the South, they're all sturdy like a dam
They fight and fuss but they should always be one
They'll always help no matter how far they have to come
They stand firm in family belief
And through thick and thin that belief they'll keep
From the red dirt of Mississippi to the Detroit snow
From the VA mountains to the New York glow
We have lost key elders but their memory we hold dear
And through life we use their wisdom to steer
So if you got a family strong as mine
You should never feel alone or behind
I'm blessed to be a Stanfield and in this family vine

© 2008 Dennis M. Stanfield

Fatherless Father

Dad you aren't ever there and we are in the same house!
You don't deserve me or your spouse
In that moment it was like the ghost of Christmas past
He's just like his pops and there's a clash
A fatherless father he is
And it took him 12 years to realize this
All the pain comes back up his throat and holds his breath
He feared being a fatherless father more than death
He's floating around these images
This the real game, no more scrimmages
Snap, there goes gravity
And he falls back to reality
Can't even look his boy in the eye
Feels like he should run and hide
Finally he says, "Son I'm making no excuses for my past
Because everyone has a choice to cut grass
It's a long road, but with you guiding me I'll stay on the path
I failed to give you the basic need, my time
I don't want to try and change your mind
But I'll let my actions speak."
His knees went weak
He said, "Son you won't be a fatherless father."
He fell to his knees and hugged his son
Dad you're afraid to be a fatherless father but you don't have to be one
Just be a father and later I'll be one

© 2008 Dennis M. Stanfield

Starts at Home

Kids today are bad, that's what people complain
And they say TV is to blame
So what dictates what?
Most times it's the power of the buck
But it all starts at home
Homes are broken and kids are left alone
So who is to raise them?
Mom is always working and daddy left them
So pick your poison, the streets or TV?
Access to both is pretty easy
Video models and gangsters are role models now
You ask what happen, how?
Broken communities
And worse than that broken families
Drugs, crime and a lack of leadership
We need to look to God for a tip
People that can, will take advantage of you
And if no one is home to lead, who they gone look too?
It starts at home with values and morals
With those in place it should cut down on the quarrel
Kids are the future, you agree?
But it starts at home, parents are the key

© 2008 Dennis M. Stanfield

Going Backwards

Slaves were bound by whips and chains
Now our people are chasing whips and chains
Look like we as a people going are backwards
We only say what's right in front of cameras like actors
We sell drugs to get whips and chains
I mean come on; doesn't any of this seem strange?
Hip-Hop was a leader, now they're walking in a daze
In a rush to that concert to hear what ya favorite rapper would say
But your five minutes late so it's too late on God's day
So is it wrong to want nice whips and chains?
Think about this, what do you gain?
The playing field isn't the same
You got to work twice as hard in this game
You can go ahead and work just for whips and chains
But you're just on the team, the GM is Danny Ainge
That's just the facts simple and plain
Let's go forward; it's about more than whips and chains

© 2008 Dennis M. Stanfield

Hardtime, USA

Hardtime is where a lot of people live
Could also be called village ghetto land where no one gives
The people of authority just take
There, for people life isn't great
Violence, murder, crime and utter chaos
The people are wondering, how could the system betray us?
The preservation of the city is more important than the people
More lines of separation, though they say all are equal
Liquor stores on every other corner
Girls can't walk down the street with out hands on her
The best business is the drug trade
That's where you got to go to get paid
Police got a deal with dealers here
They go out together and have a beer
City leaders just look the other way
Katrina happens every other day
Got you working just enough not to have full time
You keep saying you gone quit this time
But who gone feed the fam?
They got you in a jam
Only thing else is drugs
But you gave up that life of thugs
It's nothing but hard times with no help
And most don't have a heart to feel heartfelt
Bills on top of bills
Feels like you can't catch a break, no deals
Everything looks ok, then come off the wheels
Sounds familiar ay?
Look around the corner round your way
I'm sure you know a Hardtime, USA

© 2008 Dennis M. Stanfield

Stuck On the Roof

Wouldn't you loot?
Baby need food and you stuck on the roof
You're the only one who can go and make it back
Telling your baby to take a nap
Tell 'em you'll be right back
Water so high you'll drown
So cold you can't move and feels like your feet are bound
Empty paddle boat found
People counting on you, you'll take any food, any kind
Praying to God to give you a sign
Bodies floating in the water but you got to keep it moving
Keep waiting for the Coast Guard to cruise in
Or the government to come to the rescue
But they left us for fish food
A store!
Thank the Lord!
Window already broken in
Safety the boat and move in
Camera says you looting
People ready to start shooting
But you got to make it back to the people in need
So you take anyway and leave
Yeah he made it back with food, that's the truth
But they still stuck on the roof
What they gone do?

© 2008 Dennis M. Stanfield

Hard

You think you hard? No
Your only hustle is the doe
I've heard of kids half your age that's gangsta for real
Won't think twice about cancelling your deal
Then walk away like they don't feel
Because they living for no reason
They don't even know the season
Lupe said they killing for a soccer ball
They wouldn't know their parents voice if called
Since 6 they been in the struggle and fight
In dark so long they don't recognize light
AKs over the shoulder grenades in the pocket
All he knows is he's ready for the rocket
You think you a thug in the struggle? Think again
These kids run away they get hands chopped off for revenge
They either killing or mining
So why you over here whining
Forget education, they learn death
And how to do it the best
Fighting a cause that's been manipulated
Soldiers of men most hated
Men who use children to further their sins
The kids become rebels when they should be students
All that shows for the men is prurience
These kids are made hard
If not, they get left alone or buried in a yard
They shouldn't have to be hard
They just kids

© 2008 Dennis M. Stanfield

Dear America

He wasn't my dad though I called 'em pops
Round the way he ran all the shops
He was like the pope
Took me in, even in my Hip-Hop gold chains, heavy rope
All the real gangsters reported to him
And when he got mad, the lights got dim
He brought me up, took me under his wing
I was living the American dream
I was his right hand, no one was closer
If he was the wall, I was a poster
Many people hated that fact about me
But more so because I wasn't the color of he
A black man getting ready to take over a white mans empire
So now they turned on me and that feeling is sour
Dear America you got a problem see
I'm only what you made me
You kicked me to the curb and told me to survive
But you only gave me dirt paying jobs, besides
You made it so gangsters were my role models
Walking the streets filled with drugs, dead bodies and broken beer bottles
Then you never reported the murders you caused
You just kept us caged like hogs
And now you're surprised to see what you see?
This is you also, not just me
I learned from the ultimate hustler, you
Your ideals and ways stuck like glue
Scarface, godfather, the sopranos
Dark gangsta sounds of the violin and the piano
If I die you die
Then it's really bye bye Ms. American Pie
Because I'm the glue that holds you together
With out me the storm you couldn't weather
But it was you who over ran jails instead of schools
Instead of us owning the biz, we built the pools
See you helped create a way of life that's gotten out of hand
Now the whole world sees the flaws of this land
Instead of perpetuating the problem teach us a craft and trade
Hey I'm calling a spade a spade
Or give us the means
Meaning the green
Poor people can't help the poor so to speak
We may have missed a generation, but the outlook isn't bleak
Your plan, we solvin'
Dear America, you got a problem

© 2008 Dennis M. Stanfield

Black Panther

Some may call me a Black Panther
Young black man in America is my answer
I was born into a culture and race
So me not getting involved is a waste
It's a gap and I do blame the government for most of this disintegration
And we are separate as a nation
We may not be voting if it wasn't for the VRA
And if not renewed, no voting that day
So back to poll taxes huh?
It may sound it, but it's not that dumb
But we're not helping by digging our own grave
Than all they've got to do is push us in, slave
Most of the youth is misunderstood like Common say
So it's up to both parties to find a common way
I say Black Panther, but don't think I'm violent
I'm just a product of my culture and environment
And I can tell you don't trust me by your facial perspiration
Around the way we call that hateration
Black panthers are cunning, test 'em, that's an open invitation
Even outside my culture I set no limitation
Call me what you want

Live to Tell

Thug are we?
Well only a few live to tell the story
It's a dead end street you walking on
And most are either in jail or dead and gone
Be careful how you portray yourself
When you get in combat only planes have stealth
You can't play Denzel and live a free life
More like Set It Off, only one recalls that night
And you think in real life yo "crew" will let you be that one?
If you think that, I may call you dumb
All the real gangsters dead or in jail
Even most of the mob can't get bail
Go head push your luck and see what story you tell
Or where you tell it from
Behind bars or when your funeral comes?
It's your choice
No one says yes for you, it's your voice
Pretty soon you'll want out
But enemies and free loaders may not let you out
This isn't high school sports kid
This to them is a way of life
The only one they know
Once you in, no stop only go
Only the people on the outside live to tell that story

© 2008 Dennis M. Stanfield

Less than He

Then came one with less heart than me
Bang was the last thing I heard
Remember were the last words
I was born with very little heart
Straight gangsta from the start
See I was born into the life
I loved the rush, almost died twice
It was all I knew
My life is the painting rappers drew
I had a dad, no mom
Guess she couldn't handle the life, at five she was gone
But because of my pops, I was known
At 12 years old I was grown
I earned my stripes, no short cuts
I was made hard and made my own luck
Had plenty girls around
But never would I settle down
Many wanted my spot but I had the crown
I did it all, what ever you could think of
I had it all; I was the thug's thug
Pushed around who ever
What goes around comes around, never
I was going to retire to the South of France
But nothing is by chance
Only saw his face by a glance
Thought I was the badest man stepping this dance
Then came one with less heart than me
Remember me?
Bang….

© 2008 Dennis M. Stanfield

41

Dudes around my way
They just want to be Jay
Live what they hear in the rhymes
They don't understand he past those times
The smart artists aren't in the streets no more
You think they worked that hard to now go poor?
Sale drugs? Hov did that so you don't have to
Malcolm and Martin gave their lives so you wouldn't have to
Jesus died to save you
So why do you want to be something you don't have to be?
Someone you're not, and shouldn't be
Because of you innocent people die
Kids in their own hood have to hide
And this problem is nation wide
You around the wrong people and you know it
You got a good thing in school and about to blow it
Because you was with them, cops looking for you
With out you, what is your mom going to do?
Put your hands up, get on your knees
You thinking don't shoot me please
But you hang with tough guys so they see you that way
You make one wrong move and it's a long day
Put down the drugs they say
No, no take 'em they're not mine
Reach in your pocket and you get shot 41 times

© 2008 Dennis M. Stanfield

In a Flash

Her whole life changed in a flash
Quicker than the fastest man in the 100yrd dash
He liked her but didn't love her
Even though that's what he told her
That lie helped him go further
She was uncomfortable but it was love right?
In his eyes he said sike
She went along despite
They made plans for the interaction
He made sure there would be no distractions
Usual night, out to eat and a movie
She just wants to be down like stevie
T.I. in American Gangster
But we would see the bad decision later
Time came and she nervous
He trying to keep her calm for the wrong purpose
This is not right for her first time
It wasn't on her terms when it came time
So caught up in her thoughts, it's over
He says nothing, making her feel lower
She don't even know if he used protection she was so gone
Now she's scared that her choice was wrong
Advice leads her to testing
She's calm, resting
Just that quick, everything went bad
She broke the heart of her dad
Now she 16, no place to stay
And a little baby on the way
No man in sight
It's going to be a long and hard fight
She knew it wasn't right, but she did it
Well, was it worth it?
It may not happen the first time it goes down
But the losing hand usually comes back around
In a flash

© 2008 Dennis M. Stanfield

Gotta Eat

Nothing in the kitchen for her little girl
And her little girl is her whole world
So she does the only thing she can to give her baby a place to stay
She dances, no not ballet
She hates it but they got to eat
A lot of eyes watching every move lustfully, but they got to eat
Private shows and stalkers, but she gotta eat
She finally meets a nice man there and they speak
He finds out her situation and explains his
He now owns his own biz
He was in her place
Living with no place
Hustled so hard he couldn't tell his own face
She's not just a good looking body on stage
She gotta eat, it's hard not being the color beige
But he's there to help, that's all
No catch or trapped door to fall
He really likes her and wants her to prosper
Make her own dreams; not on someone else's team or roster
You do what you got to do to eat
He was once a drug dealer in the street
He knew the looser that left her alone
She didn't deserve that heart burn
And she would've done anything for her baby
Can't stand to see a beautiful black woman go to waste
Not waste, but letting her real dreams dry up like paste
All she needs is to see success, get a taste
It happen to her as it did him
She didn't need fast money to feed them
The old life she had, now she's beat
It isn't over though, still gotta eat

© 2008 Dennis M. Stanfield

Reality

Are we living in reality?
If so, is it our reality or someone else's?
What is reality?
Reality is the quality or state of being, actual or true
Reality is the domain of actual or practical experience
So one mans reality may not be another's
Reality is Bush's approval rating
I do know reality is different for our troops than what Bush says
Reality is drugs and poverty
Reality is a little girl getting raped
Reality is a little boy getting killed over shoes
Reality is hatred and racism
Reality is we are lucky to be Americans
Reality is children in Africa with flies around their mouths
Children walking miles to get fresh water
Children working diamond mines and getting just enough not to die
Reality is we can't help them if we don't help us
But it seems as though we can
Reality is the response time to Katrina
And the government is giving us a different reality
On the news all we see is a bad reality
What about the good?
We need to learn the reality principle or there will be no reality
The principle is basically awareness to adjust to the changing environment
Are we living in someone else's reality?
Find out and make your own reality

© 2008 Dennis M. Stanfield

She Cries

When she cries it rains
So the whole world feels her pain
You can tell when it's sadness or joy though
Flooding rain or the misty kind with a rainbow glow
Rain to erode hillsides or help plants grow
When she cries the world cries
Like saying final goodbyes
To a special loved one who rises to the skies
She cries yet we continue to ignore
Like her crying we locked behind a door
She's crying to us, why don't we listen?

Out

Billions of people in the world and she feels excluded
Like she's good minerals taken out the air, polluted
She stands in back, feeling alone
When kids walk past they say go home
Is she so different?
Why aren't her spirits lifted?
She's just as pretty as they are
So why does she seem so far?
Because she doesn't think like they do
She doesn't follow what the popular groups do
Because she has her own mind they shut her out
But she can hold her head high with out a doubt
She's an outcast and no one can see the truth
How fickle are our youth
Her life is like a joke she doesn't get
Everyone just laughs when alone she sits
This type of exclusion and loneliness can't be explained
The type that makes her feel ashamed
Maybe you can find out
Find out why she's left out

© 2008 Dennis M. Stanfield

Statistic

I'm 23, black and not a statistic
Now-a-days that's not realistic
Prisons over run with blacks
You got to shake your head at that
Are they targeting young brothers for crime?
Or are young brothers dumb as a pocket of dimes?
I would say a combination
They playing into authorities hands, time they wasting
I'm just trying to reach out and touch the kids like a Catholic dude
But not to be rude
Just get my point
And I would say a good point
Poor people are just numbers in this kingdom
And I've heard there's a price for freedom
I'm not a number on some old guy's stat sheet, neither are my brothers
But our friends will, among others
Don't worry when I reach at my waist it's not what you think it'll be
So after you get up off the ground you'll see
My pad and my pen or my phone
To put these thoughts out to contact your dome
This place is the new Rome
They filling up the jail to meet quota
Turns my face green like Yoda
That's gross
And that isn't the worse
We helping trying to be thugs
So it's easy for a good apple to get swept under the rug
That won't be me
My eyes are open, I can see

© 2008 Dennis M. Stanfield

He, She and Them

He has it all
He has it in his mind to ball
He doesn't have the right people around
He looses one dime they're no where to be found
He's all alone
He didn't learn a skill so he's back at moms home
He misses the life style so much; he puts one to the dome

She is a star in the making
She feeds off people hating
She doesn't care who she rubs wrong
She thinks this video is her break, but they're playing her like a pawn
She's in someone's bedroom
She took the fast road where she thought dreams come true
She wanted to take it back but he holds her breath till she's blue

Them, they are outcasts
Them, they can't see past their rags
Them, they are hungry
Them, they're still hungry
Them, they are happy
Them, they never had much, but they're happy
Them, still not much; but they have each other, and they're happy

© 2008 Dennis M. Stanfield

Excuses

"I'm from the hood" is an excuse
Point has been beat over the head, abuse
Yeah everyone has a head start
But you still have a role to play, a part
You not the only one to come from the bottom
You not the only one to see a friend one day, next they shot him
Poverty is a way of life to most of us
Bad credit, bills, debt, loans, all ways to trap us
But playing into their hands isn't smart
And taking back our community is a start
Stop using the hood as an excuse
You're good with numbers and weights, put that to use
Any education is a plus
Business smarts and street smarts is a must
With this new age of technology
To succeed you really have every possibility
Stop using excuses, people tend to want to lend a hand
You can ask for help using your own plan
Its tough enough trying to get ahead
Put down the gun and pick up a book instead
Anybody can be a thug but not all dads are fathers
You yelling racism, so why bother
But you aren't doing anything to claim that
You still in the same situation you were five years ago, you whack
Climb the success ladder, how about that
Then maybe you have an argument that's intelligent
But other than that your excuses are irrelevant

© 2008 Dennis M. Stanfield

Justified Anger

My anger is justified today
So far I've been supportive of around my way
But now it's too much
People around you, you can't even trust
Your own "people" shoot you and rob you
Who do they think they are? Who?
I'm about ready to give up on these punks
They want to be thugs, chumps
Yeah the government made it bad on the hood
But these little dudes aren't misunderstood
At least not to me
Through that fake thug I see
I cared, but now I care less
I'm not gone be bothered by the stress
Yeah I said it; just give them a craft and a trade
But they so deep in this way of life that it won't fade
How do you help people that keep robbing you?
I'm done, wash my hands and I'm through
I was defending these dudes when my pops said they bad
I just thought maybe they needed a brother or a dad
But when a gun is put his face
All that "I want to help" goes out in space
Like someone talked bout my momma, them fighting words
All that peaceful talk is kicked to the curb
Anger, hate whatever you want to call it
All that, I'm feeling it
Put me in a closed room with them for 5 minutes time
He'll come out talking like a mime
I know I shouldn't hate cause of who I believe in
But just the thought of revenge gives me a little grin
Am I wrong for thinking about that danger?
Or do I have justified anger?

© 2008 Dennis M. Stanfield

Surface Dwellers

As I'm underneath and look up at these surface dwellers
Scared to come down, yellow as old yeller
I see the fear of new things in them
Walking round like zombies from am to pm
They are all faceless
In a world so spacious
But they know nothing of it
It's a blinding light and they can't see above it
Just move it, right?
But it's not as easy as flying a kite
All they do is worry about the surface and nothing else matters
But they have a feast of platters
And its all underneath and going bad
Imagine all the great times they could've had
If they would've looked inside themselves
But their souls are stacked on shelves
They can't even be reached by letters
Now they're just surface dwellers
It's what's underneath and inside that count
Not your makeup or weight amount
Look below the surface

© 2008 Dennis M. Stanfield

Back My Way

It's been dark round me for so long
I really couldn't tell you what's wrong
The lights out and the path is dark
I'm looking for a rock to at least give a spark
With no sunlight I feel like I'm losing myself
Love and friendships have been put on the shelf
I don't even know what fun is anymore
I just float back and forth like water on the beach shore
Sitting back waiting to see what God has in store
I can start to walk alone and blind if I wanted
But what do I know, this path could be haunted
So I got my suntan lotion and good shades on
Waiting on the sun to shine back my way

© 2008 Dennis M. Stanfield

Dealer:

Part II

Dealer

Hey, pssssst
What you need, I got it
Blue, red, black, yellow, I got it
You know you want it
You know you need it
Your local library don't got these
Never before read books on Dr. King
Poetry, history, science, religion; what you need?
I got more than you can read
I'm trying to open your mind today
Its Friday, you ain't got no job; I'm a get you high today
Once you pick it up, you won't put it down
I got something for you to wrap your head around
This a book about Nat Turner with no title
Or I got James Earl Jones reading the bible
You didn't know? I got audio too
Bam! Right out the blue
You want to go on a ride? I can take you there
What do you have to fear?
If it's really good you'll start to see things
Like you're flying with the red tails and you got wings
Oh I'm sorry that was a free bee
Red tailed planes were the boys from Tuskegee
When you mention what I'm talking about you get crazy looks
Don't do paper? Get e-books
This information right here, this right here; I'm trying to get you hooked fore show
I'm you're neighborhood dealer… but keep that on the low

© 2008 Dennis M. Stanfield

Poetry Man

I can be called the poetry man
Taking all your thoughts and putting them in a pen
Then spreading them out nice
Throwing in my own spice
If it were music, call it a sound track to life
My poetry connects your hand to the kite
It's family on Thanksgiving Day
When your mate looks at you in that special way
I'm building a bridge between generations
Kind of like education
The youth need to know where they came from
Where they're going, the elders need to come
I don't see my poems as just poems
I make all of them hit home
Strike some emotion deep inside
Take you on an emotional roller coaster ride
The highs and lows of life
The good, the bad despite
This poetry man tries to keep it real
But there are different turns to the wheel
There are different emotions to every person
I try to touch them all with out cursing
Follow me and take my hand
Yes, I'm the poetry man

© 2008 Dennis M. Stanfield

Brain Storm

Get your umbrellas out, the kid about to brain storm
But turn them up side down cause it's against the norm
I want you to catch the ideas I'm showering you with
In every drop there is a positive tip
I don't know exactly who I'm speaking to
But one thing is for sure I'm talking to you
You with the mountain you feel you can't climb
You that's always in a rush to waste time
And you who can't see the future because of what you left behind
Why dwell in the past, when each day is new?
And wouldn't it feel good to look back and see how you grew?
Get it? You need rain to grow
Trials and troubles, you know how they go
Hope you catch the moral of the story, we all make mistakes
But you live and learn and that idea makes life great
Where you come from can mold you, but who you are should make you
If you're around good people you become them and they you
I wouldn't lie, everything I say is true
Why be proud to be a follower or just apart of the crowd?
Why not be a leader and set the tone of that crowd?
So now the storm is passing and you didn't even get wet
But the question is; is your umbrella full from what you were to catch?

© 2008 Dennis M. Stanfield

Complex Thoughts

I just want y'all to see my thought in the mode of attack
And my Roots run deep so it keeps my Thought Black
Don't be in a rush to fall into a trap
I'm just trying to turn your winter to summer
You're a bug in front of a hummer
But enough bugs cover the windshield
Then maybe the beast will stop and yield
You're more than the stereotype, they just have to peel
Away the cover to get the real
See where I'm headed?
I'm not just running around like a chicken beheaded
On the path of empowerment
Just read the letter how it's sent
What does it mean to you?
To yourself be true
Maybe complicated but ponder those thoughts
Inside and out I'm black like Goths
Learn from your mistakes so you won't miss the cut off man
Because even if you got a cannon you can over throw the stands
Then what you meant, meant something different
Just to be heard is your aim, isn't it?
I'm trying to help you pay attention for free
Because my inspiration comes with no fee
And also a life time guarantee
You try and hide these thoughts like a pimple
But complex can be simple
They told you to run through life and cut out your eyes
But that's when Jesus rise
You can't go through this blind folded
Sit and watch the wrong, hands folded
You can fight with the words you say
You can't be lucky all the time, but you can be smart everyday
I'm trying to flood your mind like a basement
Don't worry you're protected by the encasement
View the pics they show, but make your own statement
You're already behind the eight ball, catch up
Try deeper thoughts

© 2008 Dennis M. Stanfield

Jesus is My Man

Who is Jesus?
The Son of God
Nah Nah. Who is He to you?
Oh, that's my man, my homie, my ace
He goes with me every where, no matter the case
The only one I can truly trust
And His friendship will never rust
He's there through the good and bad
When I'm happy or sad
Even when I doubt Him
He's with me even then
That's my road dog, my travel pal
Because every trip I've been on, He's been on every mile
No one is as real as He is
You know what kind of sacrifice that is?
He's the friend I can tell my lies to and not feel ashamed
What's even better is He'll take the blame
What a friend I have indeed
One who helps suppress my selfish pride and greed
Even when I make mistakes that I know I shouldn't
He reminds me He paid the price, the pain He took it
No one compares
I don't care if you give me an evil stare
About my Friend I'll always share
So who is He to you?
I know who He is to me

© 2008 Dennis M. Stanfield

Message in a Bottle

This is my message, if I were to send
Rolled up nicely, no creases, no bends
On a nice heavy paper, not that flimsy stuff
Because in the ocean, the seas are rough
But who ever you are listen to my words
Not all "geeks" are nerds
If this reaches you, I beg you to live
And when ever you receive, give
Life is short, don't live in regret
Do what you can to make your life the best
I'm not calling for help, a SOS
I'm sending a message of hope
Its never over, you can still clean up with soap
Good friends and family are key
Take off your sun glasses, open your eyes and see
Be your brother's keeper, if not for the pleasure for the principle like Janet
Make someone in need three handed
The kids are not worth giving up on
They need guidance and a positive group to join
So if you receive this message in a bottle, read it and set it back out
To send a message of hope out on a different route

© 2008 Dennis M. Stanfield

My Father's Time

This is not the time of my father
But there are still things to him that are a bother
There is no real threat of slavery
But there are still many things to waiver me
My dad remembers what most have forgot
Now-a-day's technology we couldn't do without
How about real racism, beatings and lynching's
Now we worried about a black player's benching
Death threats to athletes seemingly changing the nation
Ali, Joe Lewis, Hammering Hank, and Doug Williams holding all blacks aspirations
There is a gap between our generations
We're moving with haste
And some times it seems we're making the same mistakes
Times have changed but old principles still apply
Lots of kids don't have fathers to look in the eye
And even grown up, that could make a man cry
My father has done pretty well changing with the times
Well, technology wise
The slang and the up to date styles, he may have missed
But that's not the complete list
Family values from the old school
The things that bring us together like a beat on pro tools
Nah this isn't the times my father grew up in, there's change
But as they say, "the more things change, the more they stay the same."

© 2008 Dennis M. Stanfield

Tell 'Em

Momma tell 'em this
Your father left, he's a punk that's it
You're not him you're you
You may look like him but that's all that's true
Just because he left, you treat women good
Treat 'em like a real man should
Always be on your hustle and stand your ground
You're the best and smartest pound for pound
Always speak your mind and hold your head with respect
Keep your feet on the ground and mind in the sky like a jet
Don't ever forget your family because that's all you got
And you be there for 'em till the day you rot
Just because your dad left don't mean you can't be a real man
And to a lady don't ever raise your hand
He's gone, its going to hurt
But get over it, make it work
Control the things you can
Let the river flow, you don't need a dam
Because it only builds up to make things worse
And make sure you stay in church
God is the only one to get you through
When it seems everyone else leaves you
He left, he's weak
But having a kid is a treat
Don't have if you can't provide
And to the back put your pride
So young men without a dad
Listen to what I've said

© 2008 Dennis M. Stanfield

Misunderstood

The kid is white around blacks
He was raised like that so he really can't help how he acts
But he gets dissed for "trying to be black"
Too harsh? Can we say that?
All he did was get raised in black culture
He can't be blamed that his skin isn't darker
And it's not his fault if he gets benefits
Check what's next, remember this
Racism is taught by parents
That's still a problem that's apparent
He's just misunderstood

And she too is misunderstood
Because she does nothing that she should
But no one takes the time to talk
All they do is yell and away they walk
Not giving her a chance to vent
And not finding her gift heaven sent
She can sing with the best and that's her passion
But they control her life and later ask what happen
They drove her mad
They couldn't see inside she was sad
Calling out for help was she
Nobody heard but me
All I can do now is tell her story
I get no credit, don't want any glory
She had a dream but no one would listen
They were all snakes, hissing
Give them a chance, all they are is misunderstood

© 2008 Dennis M. Stanfield

Black Kiss

Black is bold and beautiful
Black is old and youthful
Black is super, man
As in hero, Batman
Black is slick and stylish
But black is also portrayed as violence
On the other hand black is smooth
And black goes with anything dude
Black is the leader in trends
It never breaks but bends
Blackness gives rest to the tired
And a fighting chance for the soon to be hired
Also safety for the wires
Black wins the game on the table
Black love lies in the cradle
From the most beautiful of her kind
The black woman, so fine
So think of black and kiss
Black unity is my wish
Man, that's a powerful dish

© 2008 Dennis M. Stanfield

Life is But a Dream

Life is but a dream
A dream out of my reach it seems
When you're a kid your dreams fill up a room
But soon they get swept away by a broom
But I have a dream that came true
That makes my day, the very thought of you
I'm getting closer to graduation time
It's in reach like the girl I call a dime
I've turned my dreams to goals
Trying to position myself to make money like young Hov
But not to be rich, just comfortable
But I'm not turning away rich!
All my realistic dreams are in view
If I'm not lazy I can do what it do
My mom and my fam by my side
Following God we gone touch the sky
Now I'm a row my boat gently down the stream
While my Angel holds my hand as I see life through a dream

© 2008 Dennis M. Stanfield

Writing in the Dark

Every once in a while someone will get it and there will be a spark
Other then that, I'm writing in the dark
But I can see my way because I'm writing with my heart
And in the end I guess that's all that matters
I'm full of over flowing expressions leaking out like a bad bladder
But kids today don't listen to their parents so why me?
I'm not in the streets; I'm not a thug or a G
What I speak may not be user friendly to them
Unless I was a half naked girl named Kim
I'm cutting the dark with a pen hoping to leak and bottle light
So the kids can see where they flying the kite
And we gone get this room lit up
To show this generation education doesn't equal chump
I'm still writing in the dark because I see the future
And the future is bright

© 2008 Dennis M. Stanfield

Wishing on a Star

I feel like there's no hope
Like I'm at the end of my rope
I'm in a hole and can't get out
I'm held down and can't sprout
So I'm wishing on a star
God it seems like you're so far
So I'm praying you meet me halfway
I feel I'm just wasting my day
Tough times on the inside
It's starting to leak out on the ride
Rusty sides and loose wheels
And the new paint is starting to peel
So I'm wishing on a star
And trying to keep par
Trying to hold up my end but it's tough
The system is against me and not just
Two steps forward and three back
What's up with that?
Lord order my steps
It is You who knows best
I'm praying to the star
That's not so far

© 2008 Dennis M. Stanfield

Past the Stars

Come with me past the stars
Not the ones driving fancy cars
But the ones you should really reach for
Get to them and you can open any door
If you fall short you're still in the clouds I've heard
But don't just talk about it, be a verb
Take action your ship is waiting to take off
No danger Will Robinson with God at the helm you won't get lost
You don't even have to pay, it's free
God will place you where you need to be
But you have to be the 1st mate, second in command
Taking orders from God you answer to no man
It's not easy getting to the stars, its work
And people have fell, trust me it does hurt
But if you embrace the stars as a gift
There is no mountain you can't move or lift
So be the best, shoot for the stars and cruise
Hey what do you have to lose?

© 2008 Dennis M. Stanfield

Scratch

When the DJs were big in Hip-Hop, that's what I miss
It was still gangsta, people got dissed
Yeah I know
I was only born in 84
But I know good music when it hits my ears
And you can thank my pops for all those years
DJ Jazzy Jeff and Premier were my best
Eric B and Rakim keep it fresh
LL's beats were sick
Over those Rick Ruben ones, he knew how to spit
PE knew the truth
And Tribe Called Quest set fire to the booth
Grand Master Flash, revolutionary
Skills extraordinary
Eric B for president was hot
Or how about a Nightmare in the Prince's spot
And you know Parents Just Don't Understand
LL's kango hat in hand
Puma and string less adidas shoes
Exclusive hits from DJ Clue
They really cared about what was said
How about cats spinning on their head
The glory days
RIP Jam Master Jay
And respect to everyone from that era that influenced me this way

© 2008 Dennis M. Stanfield

M&M

The M&M twins of the civil rights movement
Term M&M, watch how I use it
Two different views, one common cause
One always moved forward and one knew when to pause
Both lead a nation of coloreds
Black as the night or rubber
We're now choking on a lack of M&M
We need them
These new leaders have no nuts
Don't take it wrong, they get knocked on they butts
I only mean they're M&M plain
They don't know how to break the slave type chain
We rather fight each other
Than help each other and bring comfort to our mothers
These M&Ms couldn't be packaged and sold during those times
Now these dudes is coming off assembly lines
The only progress is turning us against us
Throwing our own people under the bus
M&M put life on the line
That takes spine
They knew what could happen
Now people frail as a napkin
We losing the visions M&M set
The powers are winning this bet
Yeah you got a private jet
But are we getting to that next step?
Malcolm and Martin fought death
Keep the dream alive and show respect

© 2008 Dennis M. Stanfield

Ali

Float like a butterfly, sting like a bee
There will never be another Ali
Not just for what he did in between the ropes
But what he did for young black American's hopes
That in its self has no measure
It's worth more than buried treasure
Everyone who fell put more power in him and the people
And when he beat the government he became more than equal
They said he was too old
But he knew he wouldn't fold
Nothing left to say, he's the champ
His mouth was big but his actions were the amp
He said what you thought, but couldn't say
He did what you wanted and they almost took his life away
Ali, the 1st Hip-Hop artist, a true poet, and a man of the people
One of a kind and never will there be a sequel

© 2008 Dennis M. Stanfield

Wonder

I sit back and wonder
If I were blind could I see clear like Mr. Wonder?
Clear like right after a storm and thunder
Because everyone has a ribbon in the sky
And how could you not be overjoyed and want to fly
Even though it may be 10 zillion light years away
But you don't really think you could get to Saturn in a day?
But listen close to all your songs in the key of life
They'll define you and through poetry of song you can live twice
The innervisions of these
Have shown me a great many things
I mean isn't she lovely?
All I do is think about her and how she hugs me
I pay homage to sir duke
And the horrible village ghetto land is no fluke
These songs and poems speak nothing but the truth
And I wish to have summer soft
As always following that path of love till I'm lost
I've met a girl with ebony eyes you hear
One who brings joy inside my tears
But his songs are poetry
Just call it spoken word or floetry
Either way, it makes me wonder
How can I touch people and make them wonder?
You know, like Stevie did back in the day
Guess I'll take his blueprint, wonder around and find my own way

© 2008 Dennis M. Stanfield

Strings

You can see it in his face
The pure enjoyment when he opens that case
Pick it up, left hand stretches out, base on lap
Right hand up and down while one foot is on the tap
Smooth melodies stream from the instrument to the ear
Look at his eyes, he likes what he hears
Look at the left hand's smooth transition
From string to string, so much ambition
Poetry in motion
Smooth like lotion
Can you catch the rhythm that he plays?
Its so good, close your eyes and you're in a daze
Some people just see the notes in the air
He could play with his eyes closed, not fair
I love guitar sounds and melodies, and the emotions they bring
Yeah my pops is pretty good on those strings

© 2008 Dennis M. Stanfield

Big Brother

I have to be careful, I'm a role model
I can't go walking around with open bottles
Just saying what ever comes to mind first
Not caring who I hurt
Or more importantly who I influence
My walls maybe thick but others could be dense
I mean kid's minds are easily wavered
Until a certain age you can't blame them for their behavior
So I'm doing what I can to show a bright light
I got little siblings of my own, but there are others who need a brother
Those with out fathers or mothers
My siblings are the best and turned out good
I'm trying to get the rest of them on the little engine that could
I'm not perfect and I don't try to be
I can only be who God made me
And use my mistakes and successes to help who I can
We got to stick together like a band
So if you need me, call on your big brother

© 2008 Dennis M. Stanfield

The Inspirations of Me

God's word
My mother's strength
My family
The idea of a better world
When she looks into my eyes
My siblings
God's grace and mercy
My father's knowledge
When she tells me she loves me
The thought of a better life
Forever with her
Elder's wisdom
My friends
Positive Hip-Hop
Love songs
My mother's faith and courage
All those who came before me
Her confidence
God's love
Hate and negative people
The children
The past present and future
The person reading this
Now you know the inspirations of me

All Good Things

They say all good things come to an end
What about life long friends?
Or marriages that last 5 times 10
And whispers of love in the wind
God lasts forever
Nothing clever
Just a fact
You can't deny that
Why think of a good thing ending anyway?
The sun falls but rises the next day
It's inevitable is an excuse
It should be a boost
To turn a negative concept to positive use
If all good things end, live in that moment
You won't get it back, don't blow it
But that's the only way a good thing ends
Only if you let it
All good things in my life grow
What's with your show?

© 2008 Dennis M. Stanfield

Love Story

Everyone searches for love. Everyone wants love. Whether it's from a mate, a friend, a father, a mother, or God; everyone needs love. But sometimes love has its own plans and you're just along for the ride. Follow this ride of love. Follow them on their ride through love and their ride to find "real love." You may not relate to this love story, but you can relate to an expression of affection. And this won't be your last time hearing a love story…

© 2008 Dennis M. Stanfield

Love Story

A tale of love and happiness unseen before
The type of love only found in the poor
'Cause they couldn't buy love
And they couldn't sweep problems under it to hide, they had no rug
The purest of feelings they had
Just to see each other open their eyes made each glad
They never argued or held grudges
They were transparent like a glass with no smudges
Open to each other
Never hiding under a cover
Where all others failed, they succeeded
For each other, they were there when needed
Makes you sick? The relationship was perfect
People talked about them, but neither heard it
Respect, honesty, and trust
Ingredients to a love story for all of us

© 2008 Dennis M. Stanfield

Roses

Every night he goes to sleep with roses in his hand
He hopes she will find her way to them
He stayed late at basketball practice and she walked home
Problem was she never made it home
So now he dreams with a broken heart like John Mayer
And searches his dreams for her cause he is his biggest hater
He blames himself and won't give up
But he is killing himself slow, like the burning of a blunt
He has to forgive himself to find his way to her
That's the wall that's blocking him from her
And every day he wakes with roses in his hand and pain in his heart
So he prays to God and says that waking up is the hardest part
God tells the man it was her time, her earthly walk had been complete
Still missing her, but with a better understanding, he rose to his feet
And that night he went to sleep with roses in his hand cut perfectly from the stem
And the next morning, he woke with out them

© 2008 Dennis M. Stanfield

More Roses

He went to sleep with roses cut perfectly from the stem
And the next day he woke with out them
Now he is relieved from his heart to his soul
Because on his body, stress had begun to take a toll
It has been a year since that day and he's been healthy as ever
He now has a tat on his shoulder saying, roses for ever
It's hard for him but he has to move on
And there is a wonderful lady and she has offered a shoulder to lean on
He sees so many similarities that it's scary crazy
But he's coming through the clouds so his vision is no longer hazy
He's ready to put the past behind him like Mel in Lethal Weapon 4
He opens his heart to the new lady and is ready to pour
Pour out joy, happiness, and love
And that is a relief like a good back rub
And she lets him know she's not trying to replace, but start a new
And he knows that's true
So they sleep with perfectly cut roses by the bed
To remind them to hold onto the past and ready the path ahead

© 2008 Dennis M. Stanfield

Baby

Baby baby baby
Baby got it going on
Baby is mean, slick like black ice
    Because you can't see it till you step
Baby got that innocent smile going on
Baby if nothing can I have your name?
    I need to know who I'm calling dream girl
Baby just smile and she gets what she wants
Men drop everything
    Even they wife!
Hey baby just that bad
Baby that fine, better watch her
    Girl that fine, isn't nothing but trouble
Baby playing the game most us dudes play
    We just move on to the next open box like a mailman
But hey, baby is everything
Look here baby I'll give you my number
    You can call me
Baby I just want to be around you
Baby give me a chance
Baby baby baby

© 2008 Dennis M. Stanfield

What We Had

It was good
What we had was good
When we were in it, it was one of a kind
First it seemed forever, how could it change in a short time?
Don't think the love was lost
Just ways changed like something with too much cost
Had to pass it up for now
Don't even know what happen or how
We could go through all the ifs
Felt like a waiter getting cheated on tips
Didn't know what to do
Then it took you months to tell me about dude
But even through that I was cool
When I was ready you weren't ready
When you were ready I was going steady
And that didn't last, maybe it was you
I knew it wasn't you
I knew I was past you
Maybe to her an apology I owe
But we connected so quick she was the arrow to my bow
Seemed right time, guess not
Now the apple is starting to rot
None of us talk as much
Busy with life like working through lunch
I need someone on my time table
One willing and able
Who peeks my interest and has that bond
One who can handle my charm
She might be reading this too
If you got to think, then it's not you
Now all I can offer is never ending friendship
Her name in big lights on my friendship blimp
If we can't be friends, that's fine
I'll miss you, but feelings, you won't hurt mine
Usher say let it burn
All I can say is live, love and learn

© 2008 Dennis M. Stanfield

Heartless

She took my heart and sent it some where UPS don't deliver
It's like she put it in a launcher, closed her eyes and pulled the trigger
Now it's just out there no where to be found
And me with no heart; how does that sound?
I'm worse than the lion, the light is on but nobody is home
I'm just a walking zombie on the roam
So because of this lady, the wicked witch of the west
The next lady will see an emotionless man with no heart in his chest

© 2008 Dennis M. Stanfield

From a Broken Heart

From a broken heart, vowed to never let it happen again
The hurt no longer stands out, with others it just blends
No longer will it be broken, though it may bend
It won't cry from loss, though hurt it may be
The avoidance of pain is the key
It won't be used as an avocation
Played with like a Playstation
So if that heart doesn't want to be with this one, so be it
It's not dumb deaf and blind, it can see it
Leave, the heart will still pump
Won't be the 1st time it got lost in the garbage dump
That's just a sign that, that heart wasn't real
To see a flower grow got to have rain, that's the deal
Something that's used can never be new, no reseal
But this heart is repaired and awaiting a new sun rise
Like when the owner of the perfect heart opens those eyes
Though this broken heart may never be whole
Taking a chance on love will always patch up a hole
So now it no longer blends
From a broken heart, vowed to love again

© 2008 Dennis M. Stanfield

Acquired Taste

I know what I want and like, time don't waste
It's just like an acquired taste
I had it before and don't want nothing different
Her love is sufficient
It's a taste like an expensive dinning place
But home made in my kitchen space
Chomping at the bit to have it again, it's worth the wait
Like the gourmet meal that's a full plate
But that's just the bait
It may taste different to you
But it's the best I could do
Some like red some like white
Me, I just like what I like
It's my taste

Rebirth of Love

The rebirth of love is like none other
Can be deeper than that of a brother
Coming into the light after being under cover
To rebirth or bounce back like rubber
Comes from the perfect one for you, a perfect lover
To be reborn in love is not by chance
You can tell after that first dance
Like trying on all those jeans, then finding the right pants
They just fit, a perfect pair
People see them in love and just stare
Happiness that can't hide behind sun glare
Don't care where they are long as they are there
There together
To warm each other in cold weather
One is a great paper, with the other being the header
But it's not all one way
There is night and there is day
To over come the bad, the hurt in them
He needs her like she needs him
The chances apart are slim
They were dead or close to dead by love
Only thing could save them needed to come from above
And to jump start they needed a little shove
A push, to come face to face
Already had a foundation, a base
All he asks of her is, "Believe in me"
Now they're living in the rebirth, can you see?
Rebirth of love, and hopefully a rebirth in she

© 2008 Dennis M. Stanfield

Reminds Me of Her

A body of water under a star lit night
The soft sounds during a soft rain
The smell of the air right after
The most beautiful melody ever played
And the words to match that express love
The glow of the sky right at sunset
The soft look of desert sands
The fragrance in the air, I can't put my finger on
The feeling of a hug like no one else's
The car I just saw that looks like hers
Any love song I hear on the radio
But most of all, Love reminds me of her

© 2008 Dennis M. Stanfield

Star

I'm looking at this star
This beautiful star
This star that is all mine
The one in the air for all time
I picked it myself you know
And asked God where should it go?
He said my heart
That's where I should start
But I want it where all can see
Because in my heart she'll always be
So God placed my star in the sky for me
My shinning star for all eternity

© 2008 Dennis M. Stanfield

Cookie Jar

Pause. Light flicks on and I'm caught red handed
Looking like a thief or a bandit
I know she can't stand it
We go through this all the time
And every time I tell her I'm hers and she's mine
But it's not what she thinks
The scene changes at a quick blink
She so caught up and it consumed her
She projecting images not there
If I'm in the cookie jar that cookie better be the best
I mean 100 times the rest
Halle Berry type
Or like Will Smith's wife
If I do I'm a take the cookie not leave my ring
That's how Jay put this thing
I'm not gone nibble at it
If it's that bad I got to have it
But my favorite cookie isn't even in a jar
So why even go that far?
Trust

Black Cat

Black cat crosses his path
But that won't be the half
I know what you're thinking
That bad luck is creeping
And this cat is cunning
Making this man willing and wanting
Stripping him down to his most basic nature
Basically making him a creature
Now he has no choice but to feed this cat
Nothing is given freely, that's a fact
But what will his main cat say when her portion of food is gone?
And the sent of another cat is strong
So now all the strays come out and want in the mix
Not for kids are these Trixs
Now there is a cat fight and the dude is stuck in the mud
Fighting tooth to nail, till they draw blood
Bad luck or stupidity?
A little of both realistically
That's what he gets for chasing the cat

© 2008 Dennis M. Stanfield

Head Lights

The term searching with a flashlight in the day time is real
I'm going through it but still…
Still it doesn't seem real
I mean, we went through our ordeal
But every couple does
And it was what it was
The love was still there
I gave my percent, isn't that fair?
Time killed us, I see that now
She's not with me anymore and I don't care how
I'm lactose and tolerant drinking a carton cow
That's how I feel
Never thought that's how I'd feel
So now I'm driving around on the sunniest day
With my bright lights on trying to find my way
Think it'll help?

Redemption Poem

I can't express through regular conversation how I feel
So I'm writing you this poem to let you know the deal
I know I had a good thing and to that concept I was blind
But I'm a guy, when do we get it right the first time
You're my shining star and all that good stuff
I am that gem you're looking for; just round the edges I'm rough
But my heart is in the right place
It just took me some time to put you in that space
I don't fear a strong woman just hadn't encountered one
So it took a second to make that transition
Believe me I'm right here
You need a driver; I'm the one to steer
So this is my plea
You can take or leave
Just think, what would it be with out me?
I don't want to think about life and no you
From a hard days work, who else would I come home to?
Only to the one who sets me free with a kiss
The one whose love is effortless
So I'm writing to you this poem
To ask you if I can come back home?

© 2008 Dennis M. Stanfield

Hello, Goodbye

She's my favorite hello and hardest goodbye
Because she says stay with her eyes
I hate to see her go, but love to see her walk away
Long as she turns to come back my way
She has the most seductive eyes and most wonderful smile
I hope she takes my heart and puts it in her love file
I would love to wake up to a hello from her
Then I would never need a goodbye from her
I hate to even leave for work
But a simple kiss from her is a perk
But I guess that's why she's my favorite hello and hardest goodbye

© 2008 Dennis M. Stanfield

Loud Silence

You don't have to speak to be heard
As they say, action speak louder than words
So when she just sits there, he catches that vibe
He drowns in the silence like an oceans high tide
He can't understand why she locks it away
Her silence, quick answers and frustrations pushes him away
Loud silence speaks volumes
Trying to interpret what she wants has him running on fumes
All he wants is her to speak her mind
Good or bad, he won't mind
Hey, to disagree to agree is no crime
He can tell something is wrong but she won't break the silence
And it seems before she'll break, they'll stop the violence
How can he get her to understand her opinion means the most?
But the space between them is long as the coast
She says he needs to be involved
But now her decisions she doesn't recall
They have to communicate
It's the only way to pass the gates
She is very proud
And her silence is loud

© 2008 Dennis M. Stanfield

Talk to Me

You think I'm not listening to you
But I am; I do
I mean I'm a guy
A regular guy, not a spy
Talk to me and not at me
Maybe then you'll see
If I have to adjust, so do you
It's more than a one sided convo, its two
Some of these things you can save for your girls
I mean nails; female products and that lady at work don't rule the world
Why you think I save heavy sports talk for the fellas?
We're together under this umbrella
I want you to talk to me baby
Just don't go crazy
I want to hear all about your day, just in moderation
Take more then one breath during a conversation
You know I had a long day also
So I'm trying to listen and be thoughtful
Come on over here, talk to me

© 2008 Dennis M. Stanfield

Lonely Bed

It's crazy not to wake up next to you
Forever left our lips, who knew?
I stare at this bed for the last time
Don't know what to say, speechless like a mime
Covers made up so neat, you liked that
Now I can't recognize it, like loosing fat
Remember our 1st time in that bed
I lay in your arms while you rubbed my head
These were the best times we had
Never together in that bed were we mad
Memories people wouldn't believe
Couples + bed = sex is what's perceived
But we changed the rules of what's expected
We would go just to lie together when things got reckless
I'm going to miss picking your brain
Or how you always stole the covers on nights when there was rain
It's now a lonely bed
Complete with two, but now only has one head

© 2008 Dennis M. Stanfield

Swallowing Rain

Tears sticking to my face like a stain
Head bowed under the umbrella in the rain
All I feel is pain
And I can't move
I've lost my groove
And it didn't take much of anything
I feel like on the inside I'm hemorrhaging
I have a hard time swallowing her suggestion
Almost like a feeling of indigestion
She was so ignorant
That now I'm feeling indignant
Now my face is indigo
With a bad case of vertigo
Awh, here we go
Another one bites the dust
She ate the inside of my pie and left the crust
I go deaf to everything outside my mind
It's raining hard, like the earth committed a crime
Drop the umbrella and step into the rain
Maybe it'll help me swallow my pain
Gulp

© 2008 Dennis M. Stanfield

Remember Me

Excuse me but you're a beautiful lady
Now I don't believe in love at 1st sight, but strong like maybe
You just caught my eye as someone I would like to get to know
And maybe from there further we can go
I know you probably heard it before and my game isn't the best
Not to sound cliché, but I am different from the rest
And what I see in your eyes has nothing to do with one night of pleasure
What I see is a lifetime that we can treasure
Holding hands walking along the beach under the stars
Watching you while you try and count those stars
Because that's how much I would love you
Don't know what the future holds, but what if it's true
Why miss a chance on happiness?
Love, honesty, trust, security and pure bliss
You don't remember me yet?
I'm the man of your dreams, a secret well kept
I'm here to show you the joy that you've been missing
You're already an Angel; I'm just helping with the wings
I'm crazy? Nah, I just don't believe in chance
I believe in God and He planned the steps to the dance
He brought me back to you with perfect precise timing
Like that needed with circus acrobatic flying
Just take it all in, let your heart speak free
Then, maybe then, you'll remember me
…when you see me

© 2008 Dennis M. Stanfield

Kiss Me

The right kiss is like heaven
Like seeing cloud 9 and your on seven
Not sloppy and wild
But gentle and controlled, and ends with a smile
The pure act is pure bliss
Like the loving touch of a forehead kiss
How to kiss, when's the right time
Out in the open or behind closed blinds
Hitch said go 90 and hold
But she can come the whole 100 truth be told
Do we do it when we meet?
Or when we're about to separate, the final greet
Kiss me, I dare you, don't be afraid
Leaving my lips hanging makes them feel betrayed
I couldn't picture more beautiful lips to connect with mine
I know you feel it, to deny would be a crime
Kiss me…

© 2008 Dennis M. Stanfield

My Fantasy and I

Bags packed, ready to go
Just me and my wife, solo
No one to please, no one to share
Try stopping us if you dare
Arrive at check in
Let the fantasy begin
She's so beautiful in my dreams
But nothing is like the real thing
The emotions one carries when trying to do it the right way
Long and hard like walking through the Sahara all day
We have a break, just me and my fantasy
She sends chills just by the way she glanced at me
Doing things lovers do, running through my mind
But really just quality time
Holding me in her arms with no time limit
The light in the room, dim it
Quiet and a cool breeze in the air, feel it
Every time she holds me it's perfect
I think of nothing else but us in this moment
No cares, no worries; all that is dormant
I just want to send her to heaven with a touch and a kiss
Something so when she leaves, me she'll miss
Give her a feeling of pure satisfaction
No need for a money back transaction
A smile is what I look for in her reaction
Oh, and passion
Catching eyes at the exact point
Knowing what each is thinking, like our minds are joint
Cool is gone, it's warm
Feelings arise like a swarm
Can you imagine?
Love is what happened
There are a lot of things to do and see
But I think I'll stay in the arms of my fantasy

© 2008 Dennis M. Stanfield

Relax

Rain drops
Softly taping the roof
Easy breeze
Sliding through an open window easing your mood
Dim lights
Setting a stress free moment
Soft music
Just touching your ear drums to massage as opposed to irritate
Comfortable chair
Soft seats and the ability to lean back into position
Soft hands
But firm from the one you hold dear
Lotion
Mixed with those hands across the shoulders to release tension
Warm arms
Eyes closed and a safe feeling as you fall asleep in those arms
After a long days work, nothing like relaxation

© 2008 Dennis M. Stanfield

Cool Night

Not bad, kind of cool outside
Just got in from a long ride
Set up the bed, ready to lay it down
Missing her touch, I kind of frown
I'm in the bed, got the fan on low
Under my sheet almost right to sleep I go
Late in the night, chilly
A dream I don't remember, but it's silly
Cold chill sets in
Like I'm outside in the wind
I awake with a shiver
I need relief only warm arms can deliver
I get up, into the closet and grab a bigger cover
Throw it on and dive right under
It's no longer a cool night
The warmth of her arms made it right
Or maybe the covers over me?
Nah, her arms in my dream

© 2008 Dennis M. Stanfield

Love Air

Welcome to love
The best place for love in the sky's above
We don't have peanuts but kisses
And we grant all wishes
Seatbelts are of no use on this flight
The arms of the one you hold dear will keep you safe at these heights
We fly at the altitude that best fits your love compatibility
Don't worry we've never had a casualty
The flight takes as long as one likes
And if needed there are back to back flights
So put your seats back and tray tables upright
Prepare to be sent out of sight
To a place called love, no fee to get there
Thanks for flying Love Air

© 2008 Dennis M. Stanfield

Love Rain

Her love gets under the skin like sores
And she has a big heart, when it rains it pours
Imagine love in the rain?
Pouring all over you with out pain
Relief like a fresh shower
Her love rain holds power
Power to calm stress
To put a racing mind to rest
To soothe and make better
Stay dry while getting wetter
Hot tub in the rain
Don't unplug it, don't let it drain
This love rain you'll want to keep
An every time it rains the process you'll repeat

© 2008 Dennis M. Stanfield

In Her Eyes

In her eyes I see the sun
Her eyes glow like the brightest of diamonds
In her eyes is sunshine
Because sunshine stares at her
In her eyes the seasons change
In her eyes the world turns
In her eyes is a place of peace
So soft and gentle
In her eyes is her soul and truth
The eyes never lie they say
Beauty lies in the eyes of the beholder
And my eyes are wide open
In her eyes joy and happiness live
Look into her eyes and feel her pain
Look into her eyes and melt
Look into her eyes and give in
In her eyes is a love so deep
And that's where I want to be
In her eyes

© 2008 Dennis M. Stanfield

Love Land

It can't be planned for or sought out
If you've been there you know what I'm talking about
It's a place people rush to but most never find
It's a place where eyes are so soft and very kind
You can't go by map quest but by your heart
For the journey that's where you'll start
It may seem to take a while
But once you're there you'll smile
And it'll feel like a quick dance
Instant romance
It's like the promise land
If your hearts not true the leaders will kick you out
And have you back in a love drought
In love land, it isn't perfect
But to keep that love is worth it
Not like the Stepford Wives
Here I'm talking real life
When you reach love land, you won't want to leave
And if you do, to get back you'll beg and plead
Being here will make anyone believe
Because no one is perfect but special is everyone
You know you want to come to love land, don't act dumb

© 2008 Dennis M. Stanfield

Sunset

The tides splash
The night and day clash
Creating an unforgivable color
The kind to make you sit back and wonder
How the sky is the way it is
How far away that bright star is
Even the birds take a break to marvel
At the sunset color in carmal (caramel)
When the sun goes down its like eye lids slowly shutting
And when they open, up the sun is coming
It goes down but never cools off
The air is so soft
Till the next day, it's almost like a slow goodbye
Its crazy, all of this is in her eyes

© 2008 Dennis M. Stanfield

Landscape

Beautiful country side
Horses to ride
This is what I see in my minds eye
Big house with many rooms
Out side the window nice flowers to bloom
Not another house for miles
I can just sit on my porch for a while
Basketball court out back
Room for my shoes, to pull one off the rack
Enough yard to practice my chip shot
Beautiful woman to complete the spot
Imagine no sirens or gun shots at night
Sitting on your porch watching the complete sun set makes it right
I see it in my mind before it comes true
Like the symptoms before the flu
My dream home some where exclusive
But it won't be, soon as I prove it
Beautiful landscape in the landscape of my mind

© 2008 Dennis M. Stanfield

Until (Loving You)

Until the ocean covers every mountain high
Or until from above you can view the sky
Do you know what that means?
That's loving you through the hardest of times, through anything
Until the dream of life and life becomes a dream
Until a man comes and out his eyes are laser beams
Or until a bat and spider are super heroes
And 3+5 equals zero
I'll love you till my heart stops
And even after my earthly body rots
Until the day is night and night becomes the day
Besides God, who can love you this way?
From my heart to yours
I'll love you until you count the grains of sand on the shores
Or the stars in space
I'll up hold our love with pride, dignity and grace
Saying that with a straight face
My golden lady with ebony eyes
And forever is our prize
I'll love you until the end of time
Or the day that me and she don't rhyme
Now isn't that loving you?

© 2008 Dennis M. Stanfield

Super Friends

This section is short and sweet. I have friends that write poetry also and they inspire me as well. So I would like to show them love as well as some extra stuff by me. So, here it is; my super friends and I...

Contents

Batteries Not Included

Batteries Not Included 2

Star Struck

Running Scared

He Writes

Silly

Buddy

Sit and Write

If I Would Have Seen Then What I See Now

Golden Waves

© 2008 Dennis M. Stanfield

Batteries Not Included

Couldn't believe how lucky I was
And how quickly I found love
She was like something from a love film
Like her touch could heal any ill
Theme parks, she was a better thrill
But I got wind of a plot to deceive
It was something I just couldn't believe
She is perfect, how could this happen to me
She's so right, maybe too right
Then I saw a glitch in her halo light
She played it off and gave me a kiss
She thought that would have me desist
But then again I couldn't resist
I smiled hard 'cause I found my angel
I took a peak at her bright shinning halo
Man was I in for a surprise
When I read the small print line
"Batteries not included"

© 2008 Dennis M. Stanfield

Batteries Not Included 2

This is a mystery
Why is he so good to me?
Did I find the right one?
The look he gives me, tells me this is true love
Every time we are together I don't want to separate
He is far beyond the perfect mate
When he smiles at me I lose my breath
And his touch is as sweet as it can be
So perfect in my eyes it's like he's running on some kind of human battery
He is so perfect with his time
This is too good to be
Is it true?
I have to look closer because he fades in distant scenery
Like he becomes someone else when he is far away from me
I got to look closer because my love is intensifying for this man
I reach in for a kiss but then
I start to see a transformation as he pulls off his mask to change his battery pack
I was right all along, he is a fraud
With my love batteries are not included

By Te'erra Jones

Star Struck

If he asked for a million I would give him 2
He's something much more than regular let me tell you
He swept me off my feet some time ago
But if you ask my family they would say he's a "Jiggalo"
I can't see what they see
Maybe he's different around me
Family are haters and they don't know what's best
I make my own decisions
Which usually starts a lot of mess
I try my best to explain that he is the one
But they turn there noses like he is a bum
In the end it will be him and I
So I block fake and phony comments
'Cause I am not them
Maybe I'm star struck who knows
But I know a good thing when I see it and I will not let go

By Te'erra Jones

© 2008 Dennis M. Stanfield

Running Scared

I wanna get closer
I want you apart of me
I wanna discover your heart inside of me
I wanna love hard with no doubts in my mind
No ifs, ands or what about next time
I wanna connect on another level
Of deeper depths and higher heights
I wanna know that when we're miles away
Everything wrong will be alright
I wanna be the reason you smile while your sound asleep
The reason, before you hurt me, your heart skips a beat
To remind you I love you and my feelings are real
That hopefully you take the time out to tell truth before lie
Consider my feelings, put forth effort and try
Try to love me back in a genuine way
Be for real to my heart and mean what you say
I want you to know that I love you I do, I really really care
But it is because its so hard to trust you
That I am running scared....

By Bryana Taylor

He Writes

The pen in his hand is like the beat of his heart
The blood flowing through his veins give him life...
The songs in his soul cries to get out
This is why he writes...
Every word that comes to mind needs to be written out
Like every breath that he takes...
Inhale, exhale his imagination
And every creative thought he makes...
Share with the world his words
Like Psalms and Songs of Solomon...
Let his words encourage, lead and guide you
So your heart can follow him...
Writing is a passion to him
Like lust between woman and man...
Like a husband and wife, committed
Like his pen to his hand...

D,
The impression you leave with someone is worth a thousand words... and these are just a few from the impression you left with me...

b*

By Bryana Taylor

Silly

Yo she is so silly it's insane
Hearing her voice makes a smile hard to contain
Things she'll do only I'll catch
You wouldn't catch it even playing fetch
To start laughing off of a look
I mean the kind of one you got to hide behind a book
Her way of thinking is special to be honest
And she has to keep me laughing till I die, she'll promise
Funny thing is, that silliness is a plus
It's nothing like sharing a laugh just between us
People don't understand how this is such a great trait
And if it's not you, people can tell it's fake
But silly is all over her face
And all we would need is us, opportunity and space
So she diagnoses me with silly and gives a grin
Know what they say, laughter is the best medicine

© 2008 Dennis M. Stanfield

Buddy

So much to say, not enough time
To express my thoughts about a good friend of mine
I call him Buddy, just a nickname of mine
You know him as Dennis Stanfield, a man who is truly divine
He is so caring, loving, and very forgiving
Will never let you fall and will always give you hope to go on living
When ever in need I knew who to call
798-5552 was the number I dialed
He never says no, he simply says I see what I can do
And in my mind I knew he would come through
I have not known him that long and only time can tell
But the two and a half years I have, have been heaven and far from hell
It's the little things about him you know, people call them perks
He does them all while smiling and being there when you're hurt
A simple text message from the number stated above
Or e-mail from the internet that makes you crack up laughing till you can't feel your toes
As you can see this man is the definition of perfect
And with out him in my life, I would simply have no purpose

By Karli Scott

Sit and Write

I don't know how to write a poem
I don't know what I'm doing
I sit here thinking I know what to do
But wait who am I fooling?
I sit here waiting for something to come out
A rhyme, a word, a sentence
But instead all there is, is doubt
I sit down and I wait, I wait and I sit
Waiting for something to happen
But nothing does
Thinking about what it could've been
And what it was
I think I can do this but then again who am I
I'm trying to write a poem that is cool
I guess I should stop now since I am making no sense
I am getting very nervous and tense
I thought I couldn't write a poem
But wait, I just did

By Demetria Stanfield

If I Would Have Seen Then What I See Now

If I would have seen then what I see now
The woman across the table quiet and shy
The woman so beautiful my eyes could fly
To see her dark, smart and humble
To know she was for my heart, an unrecoverable stumble
To see her in the moment the future and present
Her very presence an infinite present
To see a friend, companion, helper and wife
To see perfection in you for life
To see us two becoming one I'd ask how
If I would have seen then what I see now

By Benjamin Shelton [*]

---

[*] *Read by Benjamin to Khalilah at their wedding reception*

© 2008 Dennis M. Stanfield

Golden Waves

Golden waves reflecting from a golden sky
Where the water stops and the sky begins is hard to identify
Out here you think just about why
Why things are the way they are?
Why sometimes life is so hard?
Times may be tough but life isn't hard
You don't need a birdie right away, take the par
Sail is up, the wind is taking me
That's God's hand pushing me
Leading and guiding my way down a path
Trusting Him, well in the battle that's half
Chilling watching these golden waves
Man, I could do this for days
Never know who I might see visiting my boat
If to do nothing else, just lend some hope
All I have to do is live
When I receive, give
There is so much joy in touching another
Having someone say they appreciate you, who is not your mother
Times may be hard, but that's promised in life
The joy always, always out weights the strife
I always work hard, but I don't always have to fight
My golden waves bring me peace
And it's like that every time we meet
All I have to do is look to the East
Instantly my worries decrease
To find your joy today…
Just find your golden waves

© 2008 Dennis M. Stanfield

Thank You's

God, the head of my life. I'm still working to be better everyday
Mom (L'Tanya) My biggest fan
Dad (Dennis Sr.) My Bar
Mr. and Mrs. Ribbins
Raheem, Demetria and Tommie Lee
My Grandparents (Tommie Sr., Christine)
Momma C
Poppa (Doctor William Childress)
My Uncles
    Alex, Jr., Greg, Ray, Anthony, Roy
My Aunties
    Avis, Darice, Sandi, DeShaune, Gene, Cynthia, Diane, Marilyn
My Cousins
    Jessica, Tiffany, Kyla, Tara, Chai, Kiesha, Lauren, Jeremy, Chris
My Fam by state:
    Mansfield, OH (I haven't forgotten y'all!)
    Mississippi
    New York
My Friends
    Te'erra(automatic inspiration), Raychl(remember OUR plan lol), Patrick(I know you always got my back homie), Uncle Dave(words of wisdom), Lee(I got you by 1 major over all!), Joe, Ben & Khalilah(y'all are great), Jamey(do it big homie), Dustin(stop plain' wit 'em), DeAntye(be safe bro), Fran(remember the kids!lol), Lex, Michelle, Anica(remember the little ppl), Rickiesha, Jocelynn, Briana, Kernesha, Brittney, Tia, Sam & Jon, John B., John R., Keesha, Ashley(rep the D), Melissa, Karli(BFF), KV(its ya boy Denny lol), Mrs. Scott, B, Christine, Cousin Nita, Joni, my LE fam, Chanti, and everyone who got the 1st book
Lulu.com

Ms. Judith C. Allen, MBA, thanks for the book reviews!

Everyone who wrote poems for me:
    Dee – Thanks for letting me sneak that in!
    Te'erra – Poetry is a gift you have and we share. Let's do it big!
    Bryana – B you continue to inspire me, hope I do the same for you!
    Ben – My other brother; I'm blessed, that you would share this poem with me and may others know the love you share for your wife!
    Karli – My buddy. What you say I do for you, you do for me. Your laugh cheers me up every time. I'm always in ya back seat when you need me... keep ya foot on the gas!

I have a lot of family and friends. So to everyone or anyone I may have missed; you know how you have impacted my life and I appreciate everyone!

Your name goes here _____!

© 2008 Dennis M. Stanfield

Granddad, this is for you…

Peace

I'm not there yet, but I feel an ease
Like a soft summer breeze
It'll be four years exactly in November
The last thing I remember is him so slender
But as I think there was so much joy
Joy that started when I was a little boy
Memories that last forever
Like when he stepped on a frog, clever
I couldn't quite handle the line and stand
He went in and grabbed the fish with bare hands
It's hard not to see the tears in my father's eyes
I lost a superhero in my eyes
I'm searching for a peace
Something that helps is that wind from the East
And Gods calming influence and words
Hearing the singing of the birds
I don't have that peace quite yet
So I'll fly around till I find the nest
Hope in Peace you rest

…Hey granddad…
I live down here you live up there, come down and see me sometime

© 2008 Dennis M. Stanfield

www.ingramcontent.com/pod-product-compliance
Lightning Source LLC
LaVergne TN
LVHW011427080426
835512LV00005B/317